George Catlin

Homes on the Montclair railway for New York business men

A description of the country adjacent to the Montclair railway

George Catlin

Homes on the Montclair railway for New York business men
A description of the country adjacent to the Montclair railway

ISBN/EAN: 9783337237998

Printed in Europe, USA, Canada, Australia, Japan

Cover: Foto ©Andreas Hilbeck / pixelio.de

More available books at **www.hansebooks.com**

HOMES

ON THE

MONTCLAIR

for

New York Business Men.

NEW YORK:

1873.

HOMES ON THE MONTCLAIR RAILWAY,

RAILWAY,

FOR

NEW YORK BUSINESS MEN.

A DESCRIPTION OF THE COUNTRY ADJACENT TO THE

MONTCLAIR RAILWAY,

BETWEEN

Jersey City and Greenwood Lake.

TOGETHER WITH A STATEMENT OF THE INDUCEMENTS OFFERED CON-
JOINTLY BY THE COMPANY, AND BY REAL ESTATE AND PROPERTY
OWNERS ALONG THE LINE TO PERMANENT AND TRANSIENT
RESIDENTS FROM THE METROPOLIS.

....

BY

GEORGE L. CATLIN.

" Find me a bower in silent dells embayed,
And trebly guarded from each wind that blows;
Where the blue noon o'erroofs the tranquil shade,
And poppies breathe an odor of repose;
Where never noises from the distant world
Disturb the happy calm of soul and sense."
BAYARD TAYLOR.

NEW YORK:
Published by the Montclair Railway Company.

1873.

INTRODUCTION.

Next to the construction of the railroad itself, nothing conduces so largely to the rapid and healthful development of a newly-opened section of country as a systematic effort to familiarize the public mind with the advantages, whether manufacturing, agricultural, or as a region for residences, which it offers ; and it will invariably be found upon observation, other things being equal, that wherever energy and capital have combined to keep constantly before the public, in an attractive form, the claims of different suburban localities, there has been a steady progress, and a growth almost magical.　Convinced of this fact, the publishers adopt this method of bringing into general notice the claims of the picturesque and fertile region, which the recent completion of the Montclair Railway has opened to direct communication with the Metropolis ; and the candid reader, if he be burdened with the cares and struggles incident to the maintenance of a home and family in the crowded city, will find herein facts worthy of his careful and prompt consideration, and which, it may be, will open to him a new vista of prosperity and happiness for his future.

G. L. C.

HERE!" said Scruggs, one
afternoon. "There! what's
to be done now?"

Scruggs was seated on a
high stool at a desk, in an
office down on Broad Street.
He had been sitting there from nine to
five o'clock every day, save Sundays
and holidays, for the last eight years.
And now Scruggs was twenty-seven
years old, and his salary was eighteen
hundred a year.

" There ! " he repeated, " just what I've expected." And
he took up a newly opened letter that was lying on the desk
before him, and read it over again, to be sure he had not
been mistaken. No, there was no mistake about it. It said ,

New York, February 28th, 1873.

Mr. Scranton Scruggs,
  Dear Sir :

         This is to inform you that after the first of May next,
the rent of the house No.—— Seventy-first Street, now occupied by you, will
be raised from nine hundred to twelve hundred dollars per annum.

Yours truly,

TERENCE DONOHUE.

And this was the intelligence which had elicited from the
young man on the tripod the despairing soliliquy,—" What's
to be done now ? "

Well, what *was* he to do ? Even with a rent of nine hundred dollars to pay, he had found housekeeping a burden to
him. His family—there were only three of them to be sure—
had to be housed and fed, clothed and shod. Now and then
there came a bill from the doctor, and there were quite a
number of little unforeseen expenses, which, small in themselves, aggregated a considerable amount in the course of
the year. Scruggs had just managed to pull through the
year 1872 without getting into debt. He had foregone a
good many little luxuries and comforts, and so had his wife ;
and even then, at the end of the year they found they had
but fifty dollars balance to commence the new year on.
Poor Scruggs ! That letter of Mr. Donohue's—who, by the
way, had done some work on the new Court House during
the previous year or two, and was talked of as Alderman in
his ward,—was as a thunderbolt in the domestic camp of
the Scruggs', and plainly necessitated a removal somewhere.

But where ? No further up town, certainly. There were
some houses to be got in Harlem at pretty reasonable rates,

and convenient houses at that ; but Scruggs calculated that
it would cost him at least an hour more every day to live up
there, while it already required between two and three hours
to go to and from his house on Seventy-first Street—so Harlem was out of the question. Then he might board somewhere, and give up housekeeping altogether. But that would
be out of the frying pan into the fire. He would be subjected
to the tyranny of some one or another of the various types
of landlady, who would dictate his diet, gossip about his wife,
and perhaps embitter his leisure moments at home, with tear-
ful reminiscences of her dear departed husband—" one of
the best of men, Mr. Scruggs, only, he would drink liquor."
And then, viewed in a pecuniary light, boarding-house life—
even if roseate in its other surroundings—promised him no
chance of laying aside any money from his income. He had
once thought of hiring a floor—or a " flat," as it is called—
over on Fiftieth Street and ———th Avenue. But there
was no privacy about that! people tramping up and down
stairs continually—the wrong people getting your letters and
newspapers—half a dozen families crowded under one roof —
" No sir !" said Scruggs. " My own house, all to myself, or
none at all."

So there was only one other course left open--to move to
the country--to find a home in one of the quiet, pretty
villages or towns which encircle Manhattan in a beauteous
coronet. But Scruggs knew but little more about these
places than an Esquimaux does of sunny Italy. He had
once taken a trip to Niagara Falls—his wedding-trip—had
visited Staten Island, Long Branch and Fort Lee on as
many different holidays in past summers, but when you
came to talk of Newark, Paterson, Montclair, or Pompton
to Scruggs, he remembered them only as places he had seen

occasionally mentioned in the morning papers under the head of "Suburban News." But, as luck would have it, just as Scruggs was revolving in his mind this idea of going out into the country to find himself a home, the door opened, and in came Mr. Coupon, one of the firm, and with him another gentleman whom Scruggs remembered as a broker, doing business a little further up the street. They were talking about the value of Montclair Bonds as an investment. "Why," said the gentleman, "that Montclair road, inside of two years, is going to be one of the great trunk lines between New York and the West. You've no idea of the magnificent scheme its projectors have in contemplation. There's a demand for more through lines; every year sees a wonderful increase in the freight and passenger traffic between the sea-board and the Mississippi Valley, and, mark my words, there's no better investment in the market than that which anticipates the enormous demand of a few years hence for facilities in this direction. By-the-way, I live out on the road myself—at Montclair. I bought a place there for nine thousand dollars three years ago, and now I wouldn't take twenty for it. The railroad has increased its value at least a hundred per cent. And then, see how convenient it is—only three-quarters of an hour's ride from Cortlandt or Desbrosses Streets. The ferry-boats are spacious, and run regularly; the cars are positively superb. We read our papers and smoke our cigars when we come in in the morning; we chat comfortably with our friends going home in the evenings, and consume less time in going to and fro than I used to spend in the horse-cars when I lived up-town. And then, you've no idea how the place is growing. Why, sir, there are homes enough, and good ones, out there for all the young married men in New York, did they but see the advantage of coming over there, and exchanging their high-priced houses in the crowded, unhealthy city for the clear, pure air and peaceful dwelling-places of the suburbs. But," and the speaker glanced at his watch, " I must be going, Coupon, to get that three–thirty train. We have a little family reunion dinner to-day at half-past four, and I wouldn't miss it. Good day. Don't forget about those bonds the first thing in the morning."

Scruggs had listened intently to all this, and his mind was made up. Defiance to Donohue, and a Home on the Montclair was the form his conclusions had taken. So he presently asked Mr. Coupon if he had any objections to his taking a holiday some day next week. Mr. Coupon didn't see anything at present to prevent it. So that evening, Mr. Scruggs, after he had got home, had his supper, and put on his slippers, read to his wife the letter of the honored Terence, acquainted her with his conclusions in regard to it, and proposed a trip together over the Montclair Railway for some day during the coming week. So now, reader, you have a full and authentic explanation of the circumstances which brought Mr. and Mrs. Scruggs at nine o'clock, one fine morning, to the foot of Desbrosses Street (they might have taken the Cortlandt Street Ferry had they preferred it), and resulted in the purchase of two excursion tickets from New York to Greenwood Lake and return.

It is a delightful ride at any season of the year, even in winter. But in the green and budding spring-time, when nature, throwing off her frosty cerements, dons her robes of verdure and attunes her strains to those which the season awakens in the heart of man, few journeys for so short a distance around the Metropolis develop so many scenes of romantic and picturesque beauty. An ever-changing panorama of city and forest, meadow and crag, river and glade, greets the eye, and nestling here and there amid the smiling landscapes may be descried villages and hamlets, half hidden among the foliage, and each marking with its snowy church-towers and chimneys, the home of a prosperous, Christian community.

So, if Mr. and Mrs. Scruggs will permit the writer to accompany them, he will probably be able to point out to them, as they pass over the road, many little points of interest which might otherwise escape their notice. There are, also, some matters of a historical nature connected with various points along the line, which will prove entertaining, perhaps. There is a good deal in having a good guide, whether you are visiting Rome or St. Petersburg, or making a little one-day trip over the Montclair Railway. Here! these are our cars, and we've no time to lose. All aboard, and off we go! off through the busy thoroughfares of Jersey City, through Bergen Cut, where no noisy, dingy tunnel delays or endangers our progress towards the open country beyond, past that busy scene of industry, the United States Watch Company's Works at Marion, past the shady lanes and cosy villas of West End to the junction overlooking the vast stretch of meadowland beyond. What a glorious view here presents itself—a sea of verdure, bounded on the west by a ridge dotted with villages, and terminating in the great pile of edifices which marks where the princely city of Newark has arisen within a little over two score years; here and there a wooded knoll rising, island-like, against the sky; the Hackensack River winding in a thread of silver through the green; near at hand a network of railroads diverging in all directions, and far away, just visible in the distance, the blue hills which mark where the beautiful Passaic finds its way seaward.

But while we are contemplating this inviting scene, the locomotive whistle announces that we are off again, and in a moment or two we have passed over a substantial trestle-work spanning the track of the Morris & Essex road, and are brought by an easily descending grade to the level meadow beyond. Away now we speed over the landscape. To the north, may be seen, marked out by occasional passing trains successively the Delaware, Lackawana & Western, the Erie, the Midland, and the Northern Railroads—to the south, the Pennsylvania, the Newark & New York, and the New Jersey Central in the distance. What a network of iron and steel these arid meadows have come to be. And of all the roads traversing them our own is the shortest and most direct to the hilly country beyond. For mark how quickly we shall reach it, Now we cross Pen Horn Creek, where a draw bridge permits the passage of vessels to the great oil works, a short distance above; next, we come in sight of the twin hills, large and small Snake Hill, which rocky, yet verdure clad, rise abruptly from the plain; skirting the southern edge of the larger hill, and gaining glimpses here and there of precipitous slopes, and great piles of boulders strangely contrasting in wildness with the cultivated scenery we have so recently left behind, we reach the Hackensack, and can trace its silvery waters as they wind through the green, far away in either direction; now on again with redoubled speed, we cross the Belleville turnpike, and note by its side the great water pipe through which Jersey City receives its daily supply of Passaic River water from the works at Belleville; now, the grade ascends and we leave the meadows; before us is the fertile cultivated ridge which forms their western limit; a ridge already dotted with cottages and villas, and destined in a very few years to become as thickly inhabited as Bergen Heights; here we pass through a heavy earth cutting, dash under a bridge, over which passes the old Pollifly turnpike, connecting Newark with the Hackensack region, and in another moment behold us at the depot at

ARLINGTON,

(6 miles; 30 m n.   15 trains each way daily.)

To the locality immediately adjoining the depot at Arlington, the recent coming of the railroad, with its direct communication to and from the metropolis, has imparted an unwonted activity and life. For the reader will bear in mind that this fertile ridge upon which we are now standing, and from the summit of which, sloping down gently to the level of the meadows on the one hand, and picturesquely to the Passaic on the other, we obtain such a glorious and wide spread view of the surrounding country, is the first terra-firma available to New Yorkers for surburban residences after they have passed the portals of the Bergen Tunnel or Bergen Cut. It is the same fertile, healthful upland on which have already sprung up, on the line of other and older roads, flourishing and rapidly growing villages, chiefly populated by New York business men.

In comparing this locality with others equi-distant from the City Hall, let us take a map, and with the dividers strike a circle eight miles distant. We are at once surprised to see how small a portion of the area touched by this line can ever be made available for residence. Commencing at Harlem, near 140th Street (which, being a populous part of New York City, may be omitted from our consideration), let us pass easterly and southerly on the circle, and we find that a

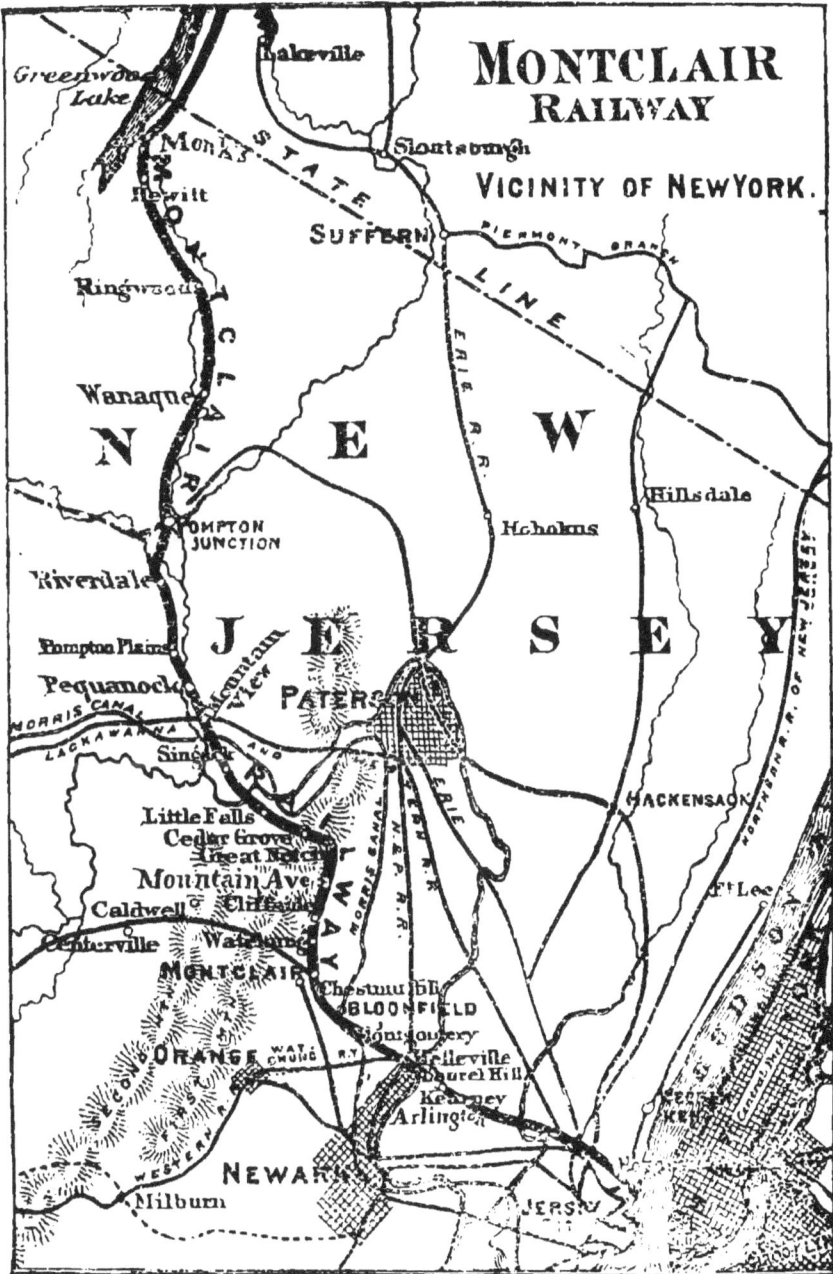

MONTCLAIR RAILWAY VICINITY OF NEW YORK.

HOMES ON THE MONTCLAIR.

ARLINGTON LAND COMPANY

ARLINGTON, N. J.

Office, 218 Fulton St., N. Y.

This is the most desirable location in the vicinity of New York for rural residences.

For full description of its advantages, see page 10

Blakiston, Hoffman & Williamson

REAL ESTATE AGENTS

For Purchase, Sale and Exchange of

REAL ESTATE

AT AUCTION OR PRIVATE SALE.

☞ Special inducements and easy terms offered in

BUILDING LOTS AT ARLINGTON.

[See advertisement above.]

OFFICES : { 218 Fulton St., N. Y.
{ and Arlington, N. J.

comparatively narrow ridge on Long Island, east of Williamsburgh, is the only locality at all elevated. South of this lie the lowlands of East New York, Canarsie and Gravesend; thence westerly the circle strikes Staten Island, Newark Bay, Newark Meadows, Arlington, Hackensack Meadows, Palisades, and across Hudson River to the point of beginning. Thus, in a circle having a circumference of 48 miles, we find not more than one-third the extent capable of being used for residences.

The localities which can be made available are Long Island Ridge, Staten Island, Arlington and the Palisades. The highest portions of these respective localities do not differ much in elevation, say 125 feet to 150 feet in height. Let us now take a trip from the City Hall to each of these places. To reach Long Island at or near Newtown, we can cross to Brooklyn, thence by horse cars to Bedford, and reach our destination in about two hours, or, for a change, can cross to Hunter's Point, and thence by steam in little less time. To reach Staten Island we can sail down the Bay, and having landed, can go inland on foot or otherwise, reaching our destination in from one and a half to two hours. If we have a house on the Palisades, we can go up the Island by horse car to 85th Street, and cross Weehawken Ferry, and walk inland as far as we please, or we can go by Pavonia Ferry and the Northern Road, and walk two miles from the Station to our Palisade home, occupying two hours time. To reach Arlington we cross from Cortlandt or Desbrosses Street, and in ten minutes are seated in luxurious cars, which, in fifteen minutes more we leave, and step out into the cool shades and rural retreats of Arlington, two miles nearer than the City of Newark, and occupying an elevation which commands a perfect view of all the surrounding country. This delightful section, hitherto inaccessible, is now brought to near proximity by the Montclair Division of the Midland Railway.

Here is the site of a great future city, and those who secure homesteads now will be rewarded by a rapid increase in the value of their property. The old fogies who are usually found opposing improvements in country places, have already been swept away, leaving a clear field for the progressive army of occupation. We can say with truth, that no locality within the same distance from the City Hall, presents to the man of salary or of moderate means so many and so great advantages as are offered here at Arlington. But is it healthful? That is just the question that the writer of this asked one of the natives whom he found living there. He was a rugged looking man, of sixty odd years. "Well," says he, "I reckon I don't look sick— if I do, my looks are deceitful, for no doctor ever darkens my doors. There is my wife in the garden, she has always lived here—does she look sick?" I looked and behold—an amazon, who could lift a barrel of cider into a cart. "There is my father just over the fence—what do you think of him?" I looked, and the old man was moving around as lively as a cricket. "He has always lived on that place, and is now 105 years old." His name was John Van Emburgh, and he has since died at the age of 107, as all the inhabitants there can testify. No argument is needed to supplement such facts.

Property owners at this point, in anticipation of the coming demand for Homes on the Montclair, have already made improvements upon a scale indicating a determination to render it a favorite home for New Yorkers. Every reasonable encouragement will be offered to actual settlers in the way of low prices and easy terms by the "Rural Homestead

THE RURAL HOMESTEAD COMPANY

OFFER FOR SALE

BUILDING LOTS

IN

ARLINGTON,

A few Rods North from the Montclair Railway Station.

☞ These Lots are nearer New York City than any land west of Bergen Hill, being

Six Miles from Jersey City Ferry,

and adjoining the first station on the Montclair Division of the New York Midland Railway.

Address

J. H. PRATT, President,

No. 25 Nassau St., New York.

Company," (advertisement of which company will be noted by the reader herewith).

Grand Avenue, eighty feet wide, extending southward a distance of one and a half miles from the railroad to the Stone Bridge at East Newark, has been laid out, graded, planted with shade trees, and is now adorned with several handsome residences. Kearny Avenue, another street of the same width, and destined to extend from East Newark to Rutherford Park, six miles north, is also opened through the property, as are also a number of other fine highways intersecting at right angles, and dividing the land into convenient and desirable sites, each commanding a view of superb scenery. To the Eastward, or from almost any point upon this hillside, on a fair day, one can follow with his eye the line of the Palisades till it loses itself in the haze to the northward; can trace the silvery line of the Hackensack winding through the intervening meadows; see every hour a score of whizzing trains gliding serpent-like in distant silence across the plain, and to the southward scan the gleaming waters of New York Bay, and the misty heights of Staten Island beyond. Nor is the view alone the claim upon which this lovely spot bases its desirableness as a home. In point of convenience it offers too its attractions, the churches, schools and stores of both Belleville and Newark being within easy distance ; and these too are soon to be brought nearer by the proposed establishment on Kearny Avenue of a line of horse cars to Newark.

Land can be purchased at Arlington in lots at prices varying from $250 to $500, while it sells at $2500 or $3000 by the acre.

Leaving this attractive spot; we hurry on toward the summit of the ridge, where our attention is attracted by the first

great engineering work encountered in the construction of
the road. For, in order to reach the Passaic Valley beyond,
it became necessary to open a long deep cutting through the
hill, and through this great gap with its jagged walls, re-
echoing with a deafening rattle the clatter of the wheels, our
way now lies. If the passenger in riding through the Kearny
Cut (for such is the name by which it is known), will take a
glance from the rear window or platform, he will perhaps
gain a better and more comprehensive idea of the enormous
amount of work necessary to complete this great passage way
from valley to valley ; this new link between the Hackensack
and Passaic regions. The rock-ribbed battlements towering
up eighty feet high on either side, until they almost exclude
the sunlight, seem to look down menacingly upon the en-
croachments which man's handiwork has wrought, to break
in upon their ages of undisturbed repose, and our train,
winding its rapid way between them, loses for the nonce its
wonted suggestion of grandeur and force, and assumes in the
depths of this lonely chasm an air of unmistakable insignifi-
cance. But ere this thought has fairly presented itself to
the traveler, the sides of the cut grow rapidly lower, the
trees that line their verge come once more into view, and
the Engineer whistles " down brakes " for

KEARNY, or Passaic Bridge,

(6¼ miles, 33 min.; 15 trains each way daily,)

deriving its first mentioned name from the township, which
in turn derives its name from the time honored Kearny
family, whose name is inseparably and honorably linked with
the military and naval history of New Jersey, and to whom
formerly belonged a large tract in this immediate vicinity.
The residence of the late Gen. Philip Kearny, a stately

structure, evincing, in the elegance of its appointments and
surroundings, the cultivated taste of its former distinguished
inmate, stands upon the Passaic River bank, about two miles
to the south, and the Kearny homestead, once occupied by
the General's uncle, Robert Watts Kearny, Esq., is still
pointed out on the other side of the river.

If the prospect a moment ago in the cut was gloomy and
oppressive, how gloriously in contrast with it is the magnificent spectacle which now breaks upon the vision. For our
roadway emerging from the bowels of the hillside, leads us
past a dense grove of cedars, which line the river, and in
another instant carries us upon the bridge which here spans
the Passaic at a height of forty-five feet. If one were suddenly shot out into mid-air over the river from its precipitous
bank, the effect could hardly be more instantaneous and
startling; while the variety and beauty of the picture so
quickly presented on all sides, inevitably elicits a regret that
the train cannot come to a stand still for a few moments at
a point so commanding. For, glancing from the car window,
one gains a birds eye view of the river, up and down stream,
and of a landscape as thoroughly cultivated probably as any
to be found in this wide world. Looking north, or from the
right hand side of the car, we discern on the east bank the
great brick chimneys of the Belleville Water Works, (whence
Jersey City is supplied), and of the Belleville Laundry, recently quite famous as the spot where the question of Chinese
labor has been satisfactorily solved. On the west bank the
eye rests upon the charming town of Belleville, nestling amid
a dense growth of foliage, with here and there a spire or
chimney peering through skyward. Then, if we turn and
glance down the stream, a scene of equal beauty awaits us,
the east bank lined with beautiful villas ; the west dotted

with the dwellings, and shops and factories which, gradually growing more numerous, as the eye follows them southward, terminate in the grand pile of brick, and stone and mortar, and the forest of masts which mark the adjacent City of

NEWARK (WOODSIDE),

(7 miles, 33 minutes; 15 trains each way daily.)

For speedily regaining *terra firma*, we pass over the river road to Belleville, the Paterson and Newark Railroad, the Belleville Horse Car Line, all of them spanned by substantial bridges, and then once more come to a stand still.

Here, then, behold us arrived at a city of an hundred and thirty thousand inhabitants, and that too within a brief ride from New York. The frequent tinkle of the horse car bell, the wide well graded streets, the long line of gas lamps, and the occasional policeman, all tell us that we are no longer in the country, but in an extensive and well regulated city, which year by year is spreading out its hands and redeeming from solitude fields and woodlands, once deemed inaccessible and remote.* It was but two years ago that the beautiful village of Woodside, forming that portion of Newark through which our line passes, was incorporated into the city limits, but since that time its growth has been magical. On the numerous streets and avenues that have been opened there have sprung up rows of attractive residences, many of them of brick and stone, and all of them in the finished modern styles of architecture. Washington Avenue, one of the great Boulevards, which a far seeing system of public improvement has projected, from the heart of the city to its remotest

---

* Some interesting facts concerning the growth of Newark will be found published in Appendix A.

suburbs, traverses this section of Newark, and crossing the
city boundary line at Second River about three hundred
yards north of our track, continues on thence through Belleville to the line of the adjoining county of Passaic. This
great artery of travel is to be macadamized during the present
year.

A ride of twenty minutes in the horse cars brings one
from the Newark Depot of the Montclair Railway to the
business center of the city. The cars run at intervals of fifteen or twenty minutes. Frequent communication is thus
afforded to those desiring to do shopping, marketing, or
theatre-going; but in the matter of the purchase of the
necessaries of daily life, the resident of this section will find
ample accommodation in the numerous stores in his immediate vicinity.* Another fact well worthy of mention with
regard to the Woodside section, is that while possessing the
advantage of being within the police, fire and mail district,
it contains not a single rum shop, or nuisance of any description within its borders. Those residing here enjoy too, unusually good educational and religious facilities. In Woodside alone there are Episcopal, Dutch Reformed and Presbyterian churches, a good public school and several private
schools; while in Belleville, not over ten minutes walk distant are to be found also Episcopal, Dutch Reformed, Methodist and Roman Catholic churches, and similiar facilities for
instruction of the young. In fact, Belleville, connected by
horse cars and by intimate business relations with Newark,
though nominally divided from it, is virtually a continuation
of that city, and will probably at no distant day be incorporated with it.

---

*See advertisements of F. Tomkins and J. P. Bradley elsewhere.

The attentive reader will not therefore have failed to perceive that as an available place for the selection of a suburban residence, the Woodside section of Newark in its proximity to, and frequent connection with New York, and its intrinsic attractions, offers claims well worthy of the intending purchaser's careful consideration. And it may be remarked, too, that there will be found offered for sale near this point, some very desirable property, available either for dwellings or manufacturing purposes. Adjoining the Depot is a fine tract of eighteen acres, mapped out into streets on the city map, having a river frontage of five hundred feet, intersected by the Paterson and Newark Railroad, and possessing therefore great facilities for transportation by manufacturers as well as convenience and beauty of location for those who build there their homes. This tract, together with a number of improved lots at Belleville, (within 800 feet of the depot), and on streets already graded, curbed and flagged, and through which both water and gas pipes will be laid within a few months, will be found advertised for the reader's information herewith.

Within the city limits at Woodside, single lots are, owing to the demand for property, already scarce in the market. Those that are offered, are quoted at $1000 for a space of 25x100 feet, and $2500 for a space of 50x150. The advertisement of Mr. John W. Joralemon, published below, calls the reader's attention to some very desirable property which he offers for sale. His office which was established four years ago at this point, will be found to be the Real Estate Headquarters for this vicinity.

LOTS, PLOTS & VILLA SITES
—AT—
Woodside, (Newark), N. J.
Cottages and Country Seats $2,000 to $100,000.

☞ My Register contains a complete list of all Real Estate offered in Woodside
☞ Plans and specifications furnished and
Buildings Erected to order,
JOHN W. JORALEMON,
Washington Avenue, (near Depot.)

Before resuming our journey, let us pause for a moment to note the scene presented on the north or right hand side of the track, as we tarry here at the Depot. The antiquated but comfortable looking residence, with its numerous out houses which stands a little in front, and to the right of us is the property of the Bird family, wealthy and old residents of this vicinity. Yonder among the trees which line the bank of Second River, are the ruins of an extensive hat factory, destroyed by fire a few years ago, and shortly, it is said, to be rebuilt and put in operation. Upon the knoll overlooking house, river and ruin, stands the Belleville Roman Catholic church, a neat and shapely structure, and about it cluster numerous dwellings as evidence of the growth and progress which of late years has been sweeping over all these New Jersey hillsides.

But now we are off again, and in another moment Newark is behind us.

We are now traversing the summit of the western ridge of the Passaic Valley, a wide plateau upon which are visible in many newly opened streets and numerous dwellings, abundant indications of its proximity to the advancing city. Now, we see on our left the cutting through which diverges the Branch to the populous town of Orange, and a short distance beyond we come suddenly upon a heavy grove of cedars, fringing at its western limit the abrupt gorges through which the Second River finds its way. Along our entire route we shall perhaps find no more romantic bit of scenery than this. The high, almost perpendicular banks of the chasm covered with moss and verdure, and shaded into a twilight darkness by the overhanging evergreens; the black, deep waters flowing between; the glimpse, down the stream, of smooth shaven lawns, and luxuriant foliage, and here and there a dwelling half concealed amid the green; the view up the stream, of successive piles of brick walls and chimneys, whence comes the unceasing whir and rumble of machinery, all combine to make up a picture, which truthfully portrayed on canvas, would charm the connoisseur.

But while the scene still lingers in the retina, we stop again, and this time, at the depot at

MONTGOMERY,

(8 miles ; 36 min.   15 trains each way daily.)

where land advantageously situated, can still be bought in large tracts at low prices. The natural beauty of location combines with a high dry soil and a beautiful atmosphere to induce the seeker for a " Home on the Montclair," to give their united claims a careful consideration before searching farther. Montgomery, in addition to her railroad facilities, enjoys frequent and rapid communication with Newark by the Bloomfield line of horse cars. Nor should her business life and industries be overlooked, for visible from the car window is a little city of brick walls and chimneys with scores of cottages about them, which make up the works known since time immemorial as the Belleville Copper Rolling Mills, one of the first of the kind established in the United States. For in the year 1813, owing to the blockade upon our ports by British cruisers, and the consequent discontinuance of importations of manufactured copper, as well as the large amount of raw material in the country at that time offered at less than cost of production, the occasion was deemed a favorable one for the establishment of an enterprise of this kind. How successful it has been, and how great its growth, may be inferred from the simple statement, that while five hundred pounds of finished copper was then considered a good day's work, the capacity of the mills is now ten times as great, while it is further a source of national pride and gratification that, by enlarged machinery and improved processes of refining, the enterprising proprietors, Messrs. Hendricks Bros., have so far reduced the cost as to be able to compete successfully with the markets of the old world. Here in this busy hive of industry are produced the largest and heaviest sheets of copper in the world, measuring ten and a half feet in diameter, weighing nearly a ton, and yet coming as smoothly and easily direct from the roller as a sheet of paper from a printing press. To such perfection has the art of copper rolling been carried by the Messrs. Hendricks.

From Montgomery, our course still lying a little north of westward, soon brings us in view of the spires and chimneys of

BLOOMFIELD,

(9 miles; 39 min. 15 trains each way daily.)

And first crossing the Morris Canal, which traverses this, the eastern end of the village, we find ourselves once more at a standstill in a good old-fashioned New Jersey town, the history of which is identified with the history of the State, and which, though now feeling the inevitable impulse of modern improvement, yet contains many quaint and interesting landmarks and relics of the olden time. The substantial stone church, distinctly visible to the southwest of the depot, was erected in 1796, and in other more remote portions of the village may still be seen by the lover of antiquities many curious old dwellings, telling unmistakably their stories of a century ago.

Bloomfield was originally settled by a part of the colony of New Englanders, which founded Newark. During the Revolution, its people were subject to frequent depredations by bands of marauders and freebooters from the British posts, and especially from the garrisons at Bergen Heights, opposite to New York. Some noble acts of daring are narrated in illustration of the patriotic spirit which animated the people of Bloomfield to repel these invasions, one of which will be found recorded in another part of this work. (See Appendix B).

Of late years Bloomfield has enjoyed an annually increasing popularity as a place of residence for New Yorkers, especially during the summer season. But now, with its extended railway facilities, with horse-car communication with Newark, and with frequent trains to and from the Metropolis passing through both the upper and lower portions of the town, it assumes an attractiveness as a place where people doing business in New York may conveniently reside all the year round. Its population is about eight thousand, and its manufacturing industries are numerous and productive ; its streets ard avenues are wide, straight, shaded and well kept; its sidewalks are generally planked or flagged ; its public square, or " military common," as it was once called, forms an attractive place for recreation and strolls, and its public enterprises are conducted upon a scale of liberality most creditable to its people. There are here seven churches, (three Presbyterian, one Episcopal, one Roman Catholic, one Baptist and one Methodist) a German Theological Seminary, a well conducted paper, *The Bloomfield Record*, published by Messrs. McDivitt & Hulin, a Free Reading Room, several public Halls, Masonic, Odd Fellows and O. U. A. M. Lodges, three Public Schools, (one high school and two primaries), one or two Select Schools, and for the accommodation of the transient visitor an excellent Hotel, (Archdeacon's) and florists' greenhouses, which will be found advertised elsewhere. The handsome brick School House, standing near the old Presbyterian Church, previously mentioned, was erected at a cost of thirty thousand dollars, and is a model of architectural beauty.

During the present summer it is expected that gas will be introduced into the village, thus offering another inducement to those contemplating removal hither. There are many valuable and eligible building sites within easy distance of the depot at this point, and the adjacent country abounds in lovely drives and rambles. The rates at which lots can be purchased vary of course according to location, but it may however be stated that good lots can be had at from $700 to $1,000, and villa sites at $2,000 and $2,500 per acre. Definite information regarding particular localities can be obtained by addressing Mr. Horace Pierson, whose advertisement will be found on the next page.

Leaving the Bloomfield depot, we pass in full view of the old church and new school house, in which are so plainly contrasted the ancient and the modern, cross by a high embankment and bridges the turnpike road, connecting the upper and lower extremeties of the village, and leading thence to the country beyond ; and then, by an ascending grade, traverse the ridge overlooking Bloomfield from the west. On the left, the eye rests in passing upon a beautifully laid out cemetery, its avenues bordered with dense well trimmed hedges of box, and shaded by a wealth of evergreens. From this point, too, one looking back gains a pleasing view of the village which he has just left. Upon this ridge is located the depot called

CHESTNUT HILL,

(10 miles; 41 mi 1. 15 trains each way daily.)

which is in reality another depot for the accommodation of that portion of the people of Bloomfield who have already availed themselves of the advantages of the immediate vicinity as a place of residence. This ridge is admirably adapted for villas where commanding views and picturesque surroundings are required to perfect the ideal of landscape gardening. We next reach

MONTCLAIR,

(For distance, time and trains see, further on)

the thriving and beautiful town which gives our railway its name. And the arriving traveler, viewing for the first time the stately churches and the substantial brick buildings, which adorn the village center, or glancing further off at the numerous clusters of elegant private residences which grace its outer limits, at once perceives that he has reached a place of no ordinary enterprise and attractiveness. If he continue his observations still further, and, alighting from the train, devote an hour or two to a stroll through the town, he will be more than ever convinced that his first impressions were correct. He will find good sidewalks upon every street; stores at which can be purchased all the necessities of daily life at New York prices ; churches representing the Episcopal, Congregational, Presbyterian, Methodist, Unitarian and Roman Catholic denominations, one of them, the Congregational church, having been recently completed at a cost of $75,000; a graded public school (including a High school in which youths are fitted for college or business), employing eight teachers, with an average attendance of nearly four hundred pupils, and occupying a brick school house which cost $25,000; a Young Ladies' Seminary for boarding and day scholars, and a Kindergarten ; a free Library and Reading Room conducted under the auspices of the Young Men's Christian Association ; a fine Public Hall, available for lectures, concerts and theatrical entertainments ; and many useful industries, prominent among which may be mentioned the Steam Saw and Planing Mill of Taylor Bros. & Co., which is advertised herewith.

This much the visitor will find that the hand of man has done to render Montclair a place of growing attractiveness and importance. But, Nature, he will find, has done fully as much or even more. For, situated on the gently sloping mountain side, which affords both a genial shelter and an admirable

TAYLOR BROS. & CO.,
STEAM SAW AND PLANING MILL,
And Dealers in all kinds of
BUILDING MATERIAL, CAOL, KINDLING WOOD, etc.
Near Delaware, Lackawanna & Western R. R. Depot, Montclair, N. J.

WARREN S. TAYLOR,   WILLIAM M. TAYLOR,   THOMAS McGOWAN.

natural drainage, and surrounded by an undulating landscape, in which no swamp land exists to give forth its unhealthful miasmas, Montclair may justly claim, in its natural advantages, an inferiority to no suburban town or village about New York. It is said to be the only place within fifteen miles of that city that is absolutely free from fever and ague, while the wonderful salubrity of the atmosphere completely eradicates the disease from the system of any new comer who may have been previously afflicted with it.

Many people with bronchial or lung diseases, have been restored to health by a residence here. The annual visitations of dysentery or typhoid, common elsewhere, have never prevailed here, and there is so little use for a cemetery, that the people have just voted to dispense with the ground which was appropriated for that purpose by the first settlers of 1660, and hereafter to patronize the more populous cemetery of a neighboring town.

So much for the subject of health. But in picturesque beauty of surroundings too, Montclair challenges our admiration. Let the visitor who would appreciate this fact, ascend to the summit of Washington Rock, and take his stand in the summer house which crowns its topmost crag. Below him lies spread out the village with its closely built center, and its villa lined avenues, stretching out antennæ-like in all directions. Beyond are Bloomfield and Newark ; further still the heights of Bergen, and in the background, standing out clear and distinct against the sky, the spires and chimneys of the Metropolis. From this rock the great General whose name it bears, watched our enemies while they occupied New York City and Harbor. Their ships could be seen with the naked eye, and their flag descried by the telescope. Turning westward the observer looks down upon the fertile Verona Valley, beyond which lies the village of Caldwell. Almost directly under his feet, a distance of nearly an hundred feet down in the rock and clay, passes the tunnel, which in its completion is to open connection between the two valleys, and afford a passage way for our Morristown Branch, which here diverges from the main line, and the embankment of which may already be seen extending up to the mountain's base.

The early history of Montclair is indentical with that of its sister town of Bloomfield, for, prior to 1868, Montclair was a portion of Bloomfield township. But with the infusion of progressive ideas, there came a proposition that the former be set off as a separate township, a proposition which was in

---

the year specified confirmed by Legislative enactment. Since that time the growth and popularity of Montclair as a place of residence for New York business men, have been assured. The population has already increased to 3500, and property which a few years ago sold for merely nominal prices, is now valuable and in frequent demand. Some beautiful avenues, among which may be mentioned Bloomfield, Mountain, Fullerton and Orange Avenues, Park Street and Valley Road are opened or improved, thus rendering available many desirable building sites. Upon such avenues, land can be bought at prices varying from $500 to $1,000 per lot (50x100), or from $2000 to $4000 per acre.

There are four depots in Montclair, the first of which is

WALNUT STREET STATION.—(11 miles, 45 minutes; 15 trains each way daily.)—At this point a spacious and beautiful iron depot, a turn-table and wind-mill (which supplies a water-tank) have been erected, and here too diverges the branch to Morristown just mentioned. This station is nearest the business center, and the more closely built portion of the town,

Passing northward toward the base of the mountain, with a fine rolling farm land on our right, and the mountain slope, here and there diversified by meadow land and dwellings, on our left, we suddenly find ourselves at the second depot,

WATCHUNG STATION (12 miles, 48 minutes; 15 trains each way daily), where our attention is attracted by another handsome depot, constructed entirely of iron. The discovery of this shapely structure gives the alighting traveler gratifying assurance that there exists about it a population

WATCHUNG DÉPÔT, MONTCLAIR.

who appreciate the benefits and conveniences of a railroad, bringing new life and prosperity to their very doors.

There are some charming bits of scenery about Watchung depot, looking both north and south. The attractions offered by the neighborhood as a place of residence are generally the same as at Walnut Street, with the difference only of three minutes additional ride.

Still running northward and on an ascending grade, we come next to the third depot,

CLIFFSIDE STATION.—(13 miles, 52 minutes; 15 trains each way daily), the point at which our railway touches the base of the mountain, and one consequently which is especially worthy the attention of those who may desire to secure homes upon the mountain side, and yet be within a few minutes walk of the casr.

The natural advantages of the locality had, previous to the coming of the railroad, induced the settlement here of quite a number of families, and the opening of a school, and have more recently been greatly enhanced by the establishment of a general store, and the opening of an avenue to connect with the Newark and Pompton turnpikes, or Bloomfield Avenue, on the other side of the mountain. In the opposite direction, Bellevue Avenue affords direct communication with Stone House Plains, less than a mile distant, where can be discerned the spire of a substantial brown stone church. Nor is this vicinity devoid of historic traditions. It was here that General Lafayette was encamped, and one, looking from the car window, may see on the edge of the woods, on the left of the road, an old house, many of the stones in the foundation of which were previously used in the floor of the General's tent.

Here at Cliffside, as indeed elsewhere in Montclair, one investing in land can hardly go amiss ; the salubrity of the atmosphere, the healthfulness of the surroundings, the beauty of the scenery, and the facilities for communication—all combine to render a large advance upon present prices almost a certainty.

Passing hence northward along the base of the mountain, we reach the fourth and last Montclair depot.

MOUNTAIN AVE. STATION.—(14 miles, 56 min. ; 15 trains each way daily), which the Company has selected as the starting point for its local trains, and where will be erected a turn table and a round house, in which the iron horses which pull these trains will be stabled over night, ready for their trips to town in the morning.

Residents at Mountain Avenue are thus able to take their train at its starting point, an advantage which those who have lived at the terminus of a line of railway will appreciate.

Here, as at Cliffside, one may avoid the expense of carriage and horses, and yet live upon the mountain side. For though there has been but little apparent ascent, we are now actually some two or three hundred feet above the level of the Walnut Street station, which we left a few moments ago. Indeed, after a walk of three minutes from the depot, the visitor is surprised to find that unconscious of ascent, he has reached an elevation, from which, to the south, he may see the Narrows, whitened with the sails of countless vessels ; to the north, the Fishkill mountains, blue in the distance, and beneath him an intervening country, dotted with wide spread towns and villages.

The visitor, on alighting at this highly picturesque point, will
find that unusual attractions have been offered to purchasers
by some of the more enterprising adjacent property owners.
Within a stone's throw of the depot, are numerous available
building situations of rare attractiveness, for persons of both
large and moderate means, while a short distance beyond,
and rendered accessible by the newly-opened Beauvais Avenue, commencing at the Valley road, on the east of the
First mountain, and extending to the west of it, near the
residence of Mr. C. N. Bovee, (whose advertisement see),
and opening some of the grandest views in the vicinity of
New York, are many villa sites, equally unsurpassed in attractiveness, and accessibility to New York business men.

Appreciating the lovely scenery, the healthful surroundings, the facilities for communication with the city, and the
certainty of a rapid development of the adjacent region, following the completion of the new railroad, quite a number
of professional and business gentlemen from the Metropolis,
(among whom may be mentioned, Hon. S. L. Woodford,
Wm. H. Arnoux, Esq., and Drs. T. C. Brainerd and Daniel
Ayres), have already secured handsome properties for Summer
retreats, in and near this most charming of rural localities.

THE STONE CRUSHER.

Four miles from Montclair, up the "Clove," which is a north and south canon in the First Mountain, and just where the "Great Notch" cuts it at right angles, are located the works of "The Telford Pavement Co." They have four steam-driven "stone crushers" in operation, and here is their source of supply for the material used in macadamizing Bloomfield Avenue—a fine four mile Boulevard, stretching from the "Mountain Top" at Montclair, to the city of Newark. Trap rock is hauled from their quarry in the immediate neighborhood, broken to the required grades, and screened directly into the cars of the Montclair Railway by their ingeniously arranged machinery. They have a daily furnishing capacity of about three hundred (300) tons of broken trap, giving employment to a large number of men and teams.

The Company's operations are of manifold benefit to this section of the country, by utilizing the hitherto useless rock of this mountain range in constructing the finest macadam roads to be found on this continent.

Mr Danl. Brennan, Jr., the President of the Company, was the first to introduce this excellent system of road making in this State a few years since, and through the tireless efforts of himself and his associates in the Company, it has continued to develop and extend until it has become the popular road of the counties adjoining New York City.

STONE CUTTING MACHINE OF THE TELFORD PAVEMENT CO. AT GREAT NOTCH.

THE TELFORD PAVEMENT CO.

INCORPORATED 1872.

DANIEL BRENNAN, Jr. - - *Pres't. & Sup't.*
GEO. SPOTTISWOODE, '- - *Sec'y. & Treas.*

PRINCIPAL OFFICE, ORANGE, N. J.

The Telford Pavement Co., have quarries and stone cutting machines

AT GREAT NOTCH ON THE MONTCLAIR RAILWAY,
AT CENTERVILLE, ON THE MORRIS CANAL,
AT FIRST OR ORANGE MOUNTAIN,
AT ORANGE AND SOUTH ORANGE, N. J., and
AT PLAINFIELD, UNION CO., N. J.

They have made miles of their road for the cities of Newark, Orange, Plainfield and Bayonne, the towns of East and West Orange, and for the Essex County Road Board.

Their roads are invariably constructed in a *FIRST-CLASS MANNER,* upon a foundation of large trap stone and successive layers of crushed rock, rolled with a steam roller.

Eleven steam engines, three steam road-rollers and eight stone crushers, are constantly in operation, enabling the Company to do an unlimited amount of work in the counties of Essex, Passaic, Union and Hudson.

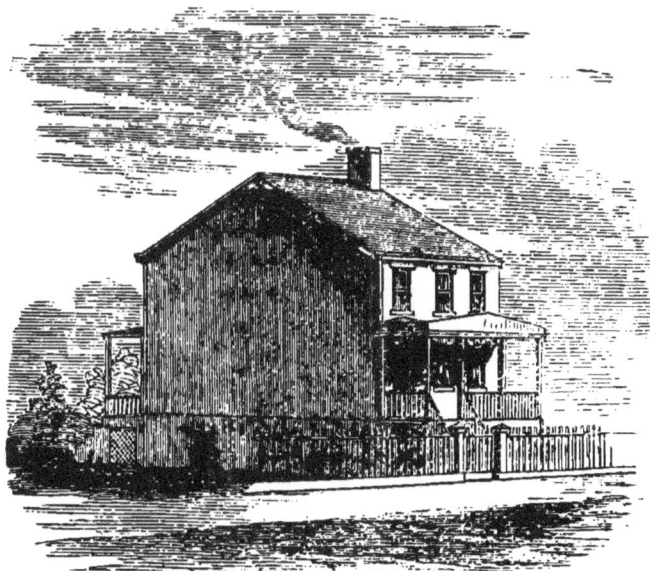

PROPERTY OF EAST JERSEY LAND CO.—CEDAR GROVE.

CEDAR GROVE.

16 miles ; 1 hour. 6 trains.

South of Little Falls we have Cedar Grove, one of the most choice localities within an hour of the great city. Beautifully sloping from the banks of Peckham river to the tops of several mountains, its wide avenues and rectangular squares, give assurance of present and increasing attractions, as its fine villa sites find occupants. The look-out over the valley of the river to the spires of Paterson in the distance, gives a pleasing picture of unequaled variety. The soil is well adapted to gardens, lawns, and ornamental shrubbery. Abundance of excellent water exists for wells—where the living streams flowing between the two mountains, will give at a future day an ample supply for hydrants, if required. The location is unsurpassed for health. The land above plotted is owned by the East Jersey Land Co., Office, 38 Montgomery St., Jersey City, where apply.

Our next stopping place is

GREAT NOTCH or RIDGE ROAD.

(15 miles ; 1 hour.   15 trains each way daily.)

We are now in the great mountain passage known as " the Notch," the only point within a range of eleven miles at which, without tunneling, the engineer could carry his roadway over to the Peckman River Valley, which bounds the mountain's western slope.   During the Revolutionary days Washington regarded this wild defile as an important point, and close at hand are dug up to this day, relics which mark the camp ground of the riflemen whom he stationed here as advanced posts to give notice of the approach of predatory parties of the enemy.   The scenery of the Notch is extremely

---

rugged and picturesque; nor any the less so when viewed from the car platform, as one moment we whirl through a deep cutting; next whiz around a long curve, describing more than a semi-circle; then suddenly shoot over a great trestle work bridging a chasm, and from the summit of which we catch a long vista of forest and hillside—then through another rock ribbed cut, and around another curve, until, no matter how sensitive or well trained may be the travelers bump of direction, he will probably be obliged to confess that he has lost the points of the compass for just this once.

The advertisement of Edward Francisco, Esq., one of the largest land owners in Passaic County, will be found on page 35, and calls the attention of the prospective purchaser of a "Home on the Montclair," to some choice and attractive sites at this point, which he places upon the market for the coming season. The visitor can either alight at Mountain Avenue, and by a ride of half a mile reach a portion (or the first tract), of this property, or can go on to the station at Great Notch or Ridge Road, and thence by a walk or drive of only a quarter of a mile, reach the same spot, comprising a tract of upwards of one-hundred acres, every foot of which is eligible for residences. A quarter of a mile west of the latter depot, on the slope overlooking the lovely Passaic Valley, he can reach, too, another tract of thirty-one acres, containing numerous desirable building sites. The view obtained from almost any point on this property is superb.

A bill has been introduced into the Legislature making the Directors of the Board of Freeholders of Passaic, Bergen and Hudson Counties, Commissioners with full power and authority to lay out and construct a public road from the "Notch" to Weehawken, via the Paterson Plank Road near Secaucus, and passing over the Passaic River at Rutherford Park, which will give a superior outdrive for the wealth and fashion of New York, and connect these two great points of interest, Central Park and the picturesque Great Notch.

Indeed, it is safe to say of this and of Mr. C. N. Bovee's large neighboring homestead properties, that the views from them are among the most magnificent to be found within an equal distance (14 miles) of New York city. To the north is Paterson, to the west Boonton and the Fairfield Valley, below are Little Falls and Singack, with the Verona Valley stretching away to the southward ; while if the eye wanders away to the northwest, it discerns the spire of the Pompton Plains church, and finally rests upon the hazy blue outlines of Long Pond Mountain, near the northern confines of the State. And if the visitor ascend the mountain to the east, a walk of ten minutes brings him to a glorious view of Montclair, Bloomfield, Newark, Manhattan, and the rounded hill tops of Staten Island in the distance. The healthfulness of this vicinity is unsurpassed ; springs of the purest, coolest water abound ; the soil is fertile, and in some places indicates the presence of rich veins of iron ore beneath, awaiting development ; the drives are unusually fine, Paterson and Montclair being each only four miles distant, and new avenues, affording convenient access to the adjacent depots, are opened or being opened through the property.

To purchasers in large tracts Mr. Francisco will sell at $500 per acre, and his offer is well worthy of attentive consideration.

We next cross the Peckman River by a high bridge, catch a view of Cedar Grove, and in a few moments more, are at the village of

LITTLE FALLS,

(18 miles ; 1 hour and 3 minutes. 6 trains each way daily.)

Situated on the Passaic River, and deriving its name from the rapids which here descend fifty-one feet in half a mile,

and are to some extent utilized for manufacturing purposes.
The Morris Canal here crosses the Passaic by a beautiful
stone aqueduct of 80 feet span, The City of Paterson is
only four miles to the north, and even at this distance the
river, winding between overhanging bluffs, high enough to
contain a river of twenty times its depth, gives in the forma-
tion of its banks, here and there rising in perpendicular faces
of rock crowned with cedars, indications of its approach to
the great chasm into which ere long it is to leap, at the
famous Passaic Falls. .

For Little Falls, the coming of the Montclair Railway,
which passes through its center, is an incalculable benefit,
inasmuch as a ride of a mile has hitherto been necessary to
reach the nearest railway station.   As a consequence, there
are expectations, and just ones, of a large increase in the
number of residents, permanent and transient, from the Metropolis.   It is to be regretted, however, that much of the
property available for residences is held by parties who are
not desirous of selling it, a fact which may to a considerable
extent retard what would otherwise prove a rapid and profit-
able development.

There are here two churches (Methodist and Dutch Reformed), a Public School, a Carpet Factory, two Hotels and
several stores.   Stages run twice a day to Paterson, and
there are three mails to and from the rest of the world.
During the coming summer horse cars will probably be running from Paterson to Little Falls, making the entire distance
in about one hour.*

A mile beyond Little Falls, we come to old fashioned

---

* See advertisement of Allen & Dunning published elsewhere.

PASSAIC FALLS.

SINGACK,

(19 miles; 1 hour and 6 min.   4 trains each way daily.)

an antiquated relic of the days when High Dutch and Indian together formed the only jargon spoken in this part of New Jersey. The Singack Creek passes through the village, which is scattered over an area of a square mile or so, and in the vicinity are some of the most extensive brick yards in the State.

Beyond the Singack Depot, we again cross the Morris. Canal, and reach the intersecting point of the Delaware, Lackawanna and Western Railroad, at   _

MOUNTAIN VIEW, (FORMERLY MEAD'S BASIN),

(21 miles ; 1 hour, 16 min.   4 trains each way daily.)

Here we are well up in the world, or topographically so at all events, but there is, it must be confessed, but little in the surroundings to woo one hither in search of a residence. The village itself, (it retains its name of Mead's Basin), is a small and unpretentious one, situated hard by, and can claim no especial attention unless it be on account of its wonderful resemblance to a dozen other sleepy canal villages to be found within as many miles on either side.

And now, for the second time in our journey, we cross the Passaic River, and at a point not far from its confluence with the Pompton River, which, in turn, is formed a few miles above by the united waters of the Pequannock, the Wanaque and the Ramapo, issuing from as many valleys, which, fan like, open off from the upper end of Pompton Plains, which we are now approaching. And here we stop at the little station of

PEQUANNOCK,

(23 miles; 1 hour and 20 minutes; 6 trains each way daily.)

Deriving its name from the township, and boasting a store, school and post office, and a considerable population living within a distance of a mile or more about the depot.

And now, looking from the car window, on both sides, we see a wide stretch of level and well cultivated farm land, bounded in each direction by gently sloping mountains. No longer do we look down through long vistas of mountain gorges, or hear the clatter of our wheels reverberated back from rocky precipitous walls—here the prospect is open, peaceful, fair; we see a landscape dotted with farm houses of the more substantial kind, well watered by running streams, and evidently in a high state of cultivation; here and there a church spire rises, or a curl of blue smoke from a tall chimney, showing where men's hands and brains are at work. Yes, this is

POMPTON PLAINS,

(25 miles; 1 hour and 24 minutes. 6 trains each way daily,)

A locality famous for its fertility and prosperity even since the earlier days of New Jersey's settlement. Here upon our left we see the Pompton Plains Church, the congregation of which was first organized in 1736. Within its congregationl limits were then included what are now the congregations of six churches. At the commencement of the Revolutionary War a liberty pole was put up on the ground near the parsonoge, which the Tories cut down several times. At length the people put up one and defended it with bars of iron, attaching it to a sign board, with these significant words,

"Liberty, Property, No Popery."* The traveler will observe that a liberty pole stands near the church to this day, probably as a land-mark which the people are averse to removing.

Purchasers of property about Pompton Plains depot will find it a pleasant neighborhood, with many agreeable and cultivated families residing there. There are also store and a hotel, while up and down the valley the roads are good and the drives attractive.

Pompton, which covers an area of six miles or more, has, it may be said, three centers of population : the first of these, Pompton Plains, we have just visited ; the second one we reach, and probably the most densely populated, is known as the Pompton Steel Works, and to reach this we alight at the next station,

RIVERDALE,

(26 miles ; 1 hour, 28 minutes.   6 trains each way daily.)

Situated about in the center of the Plains, and surrounded by charming meadow lands, rising here and there into attractive elevations for building sites. But, as is previously intimated, Riverdale is chiefly important as the point at which passengers alight for the quite populous village lying half a mile to the south, under the shadow of Colfax Mountain, and within sound of the unceasing roar of the Pung-tong Falls of the Ramapo, which, here emerging from the seclusion of Arrareek Lake, through which it finds its way, hurries forward down the valley to join its sister streams on their march to the sea.

In addition to the steel works, which employ a large force of workmen, there are here an Episcopal church, a good hotel, a post-office, several stores, and a very handsome iron

---

* Memorial Sermon of Rev. J. V. N. Schenk, Nov. 22, 1871.

bridge, spanning the Ramapo. Hard by is the ancient residence of the Colfax family, which in revolutionary days,
furnished the country a gallant commander for General
Washington's body-guard, and in modern times a Vice-Pres-
ident. In the little square enclosure, adjoining the family
mansion, can be seen the simple shaft which marks the last
resting place of the former.

From Riverdale diverges on our left, a track by which
through trains can run direct to Bloomingdale, and thence
on over the main line, instead of going around by way of
Pompton Junction.

The third center of population is known as Pompton
Church, and to reach this we must alight at the station known
as

POMPTON,

(27 miles; 1 hour, 30 minutes. 6 trains each way daily.)

where our road crosses the Bloomingdale turnpike, on which
a short distance to the right stands the church referred to,
together with a few dwellings and an hotel. But, we scarcely
stop here, for a few hundred feet ahead of us is the double
bridge spanning the noisy Pequannock, and on its further
side is

POMPTON JUNCTION,

(27½ miles; 1 hour, 32 minutes. 6 trains each way daily.)

where we cross the line of the New Jersey Midland, and en-
ter the portals of the picturesque Wanaque Valley. To the
right stands Ramapo Mountain; to the left, Federal Rock,
twin pillars, guarding the entrance to a region so comparatively unknown, and yet so wildly beautiful.

Here at the Junction there appears to be prospect of considerable development. A hotel to accommodate fifty guests is being built, one or two streets have been cut and graded, and several small dwellings put up, and the Company propose to erect, at the intersecting point of their two lines, a handsome depot for their joint use.

And we now are hastening up the Wanaque, (sometimes erroneously written Wynockie) Valley, the same wild region which one reaches by taking the Sterling Railway, from Sterling Junction on the Erie Railway. Passing up this valley, which seems to grow narrow as we advance, we see here and there old stone houses marking the homes of the descendants of those pioneers who first dared penetrate and establish their homes in this secluded spot; and presently we cross the Wanaque River, and stop at the village of

WANAQUE,

(31 miles; 1 hour, 42 min.   4 trains each way daily.)

a small scattered settlement lying principally on the west, or left hand side of the track, and boasting a Methodist church, a store or two, and a public school. About two miles west of the village, on High Point Mountain, are the Wanaque mines. There is also a small mine about half a mile northeast of the station.

A little, perhaps not over three quarters of a mile, further up the valley, we reach

MIDVALE,

(31¾ miles; 1 hour, 52 min.   4 trains each way daily)

a station better known to the residents of the country for twenty miles around as " Coon Tice's." Ask a man in the

Wanaque Valley, the way to Midvale, and ten to one he'll tell you there's no such place ; but there's not a man, woman or child from Ringwood Furnace down to Pompton Plains, but can point straight to Coon Tice's, no matter what hills and brakes intervene.

Coon Tice, Esq., has kept a tavern here since a week or two after the date on which Columbus discovered America ; and no ordinary tavern either, but a good old time hostelry, where genuine cheer for man and beast can be found winter and summer. Does a sleighing party start out from Montclair on a moonlight night in winter ? To Coon Tice's they go. Do the Paterson City Fathers determine upon an official spree ? Roast Pig at Coon Tice's. In fine, of all landlords in all Jersey, none more enticing than Tice.

Well, here is his place. Look out the window here on the left. A number of barns and stables, and behind them the house, a rather more pretentious frame building than most we have thus far seen in the valley. There is an air of cultivation visible, too, in the presence of a birdhouse or two, and neat fences. In fine, without affectation or ceremony, the people at Coon Tice's always make the visitor comfortable, and send him away with a joyful countenance and an appetite knocked to splinters.

GO AND SEE COON.

Half a mile beyond his haven of rest is another one of another kind, the Midvale Methodist Church, a modest edifice, standing within a few feet of the track. If it were Sunday, we should, doubtless, in passing, see horses and wagons tied up at all the trees and fences near by, with groups of half-grown youths lounging about the front steps ; or, perhaps, it might be our good fortune to catch a faint wafting of the quaint harmonies of the choir, or the sound of the exhorter within.

But next we cross Stony Road, a highway well named if ever one was, and come afterward in full view (on the left hand side) of Furnace Pond, formed by the widening of Wanaque River at this point. In olden times, a furnace in operation at the lower end of this pond gave it the name it still retains.

And now the mountains on our left rise in successive knolls or points to a surprising height, giving a new grandeur to the scenery. Winbeam and Bear Mountain in turn rear their wild crests, while beyond them are Green Hill and Tory House Hill, the latter named, presumably, from some interesting revolutionary incident. While we are admiring the vastness of these long declivities, a glance to the right suddenly discloses the valley opening off on that side into a wide and comparatively level tract, through which flows the Ringwood River to join the Wanaque. And now, here we are at

RINGWOOD, or BOARDVILLE,

(35 miles, 2 hours; 4 trains each way daily.)

The last name to this immediate vicinity is the most appropriate, for hereabout are the possessions of the Mr. Board, in whose honor it was bestowed. But here, too, diverges the branch road to Ringwood, a little mining village of 500 inhabitants, three miles distant, situated within half a mile of the State Line, and known by many as the place of residence of Messrs. Abram S. Hewitt and Edward Cooper, the proprietors of the mines, and whose dwellings, though located here in this comparatively remote spot, are marvels of elegance and completeness.

The Ringwood Branch transports large quantities of coal to and ore from the Ringwood Works, the only outlet of which hitherto has been the Sterling Railway, which, operating in connection with the Erie, has furnished but one train per day.

Leaving Boardville, our course turns off to the north-west, and we skirt the mountain side, looking down upon some charming sylvan scenes. Yonder, in the valley, embowered in foliage, can be seen a comfortable residence of the olden time, part of it stone, and constructed a hundred years ago. Think of the manhood and adventure it required to come and build a home over a century ago in this wild region to which the railroad has only now brought its welcome clatter. Yet those walls are suggestive of comfort and good cheer, and are occupied by Messrs. Schermerhorn of New York, who have purchased a large and valuable tract just above, with the intention of developing at once its wealth in lumber and minerals, and of utilizing for manufacturing purposes the fine water power furnished by the Wanaque; just above we shall see where they have already constructed a dam and erected a mill, and where, too, on yonder mountain, whole acres have been clean shaven of timber by the axes of their sturdy workmen. And, look, here we are at

MONK'S,

(38 miles; 2 hours, 10 min. 4 trains each way daily.)

deriving its name from the occupant of the neighboring farm houses. Here a much traversed county road crosses the track, thus affording easy railway communication for the population of the adjacent country. For a while this was the terminus of the road; but the completion of the heavy rock cutting just beyond opens the way now to

RINGWOOD FURNACE,

(41 miles; 2 hours 15 min.   4 trains each way daily.)

Where there is also quite a mining village and a post office, and whence stages connect for

GREENWOOD LAKE,

(43 miles; 2 hours 30 min.   4 trains each way daily.)

Have you, reader, ever been to Greenwood Lake? Every year the number of pilgrims to this sylvan Mecca has been increasing; have you helped to swell the throng? For a long time passengers had to reach it at the expense of a three hours' ride on the Erie cars to Monroe, and thence stage it over the mountains for nine or ten miles. But they came, even in spite of that. Then last year the Midland carried them to Newfoundland, and so saved them about an hour's staging. With those facilities, the crowd of visitors to the Lake increased perceptibly. But what will be the rush this summer, with the Montclair Railway cars running direct to the Lake itself, and transporting sweltering passengers from New York and Newark, in a comparatively short ride, to this most delightful of mountain lakes? For, weary of the threadbare joys of Long Branch, Lake Mahopac and Fire Island, the wealth and fashion of New York will eagerly pounce upon this last and most beauteous pearl in the coronet of adjacent summer resorts.

But here in the mountain solitudes, the arriving traveler will find amid the most romantic and varied surroundings, all the comforts and appliances of civilized life. For years past, knowing tourists have made Greenwood Lake an indispensable part of their summer trip ; but how few there are comparatively who have really known what a charming place it is, this cool, quiet lake, sparkling like a jewel in the emerald setting of the mountain top. How few, on reaching its wooded marge, will be prepared to find in waiting a lively little steamboat, (brought up in pieces all the way from New York), with steam up and all ready to convey them to their destination. There are accommodations for hundreds of guests, good pure water, bracing air, glorious scenery, fine drives, boating, bathing, fishing and flirting, and all these too within daily business distance of New York. To such a. terminus as this, then, does our newly completed railway bring the traveler, carrying him over no hum-drum, common-place section of country, but through a scenery as varied and beautiful as any in the world ; past cities, over rivers, through mountain gorges, across smiling, peaceful landscapes, and, finally, landing him here on the mountain top at the verge of a lake as beautiful as Como or Maggiore. And hard indeed to be pleased must he be, who, desiring a home in the rural regions whither daily he may fly from the dust and turmoil of city business life, cannot somewhere or another in this panorama choose a spot where,

> " Full in the center of some shady grove,
> By nature formed for solitude and love,
> On banks arrayed with ever blooming flowers,
> Near beauteous landscapes, or by roseate bowers,"

for the remainder of his days he may dwell under his own vine and fig tree, and with Mr. and Mrs. Scruggs, bless the day that he set out to look for a " HOME ON THE MONTCLAIR."

'APPENDIX A.

From the New York Times, December 30, 1872.

It was in the month of May when those old emigrants from Connecticut pitched their tents on the site of the present large and thriving city of Newark. Had they arrived later in the year they would probably have chosen some favored spot for their future home which was not quite in so close proximity to the marshes and their annual Autumn pestilence in the shape of mosquitoes. But in spite of marshes and mosquitoes, Newark has grown, as the old ladies say, beyond all knowledge, and with a rapidity, of late years which throws the growth of New York and Brooklyn into the cold shade. In twelve years the population of the city has more than doubled, (in 1858 it was estimated at 60,000, at the beginning of this year it was estimated at 125,000,) factories and mills of all descriptions have sprung up, others are in course of erection, banks and wholesale trade are coming to the front, and Newark dives its hands deep down into its well-filled pockets, and looks complacently around with an air of satisfaction and honest pride.

Capt. Robert Treat. of Milford, and Parson Abram Pierson, of Branford, the first with a following of forty-one, the second with a company of twenty-three persons, took possession of their new settlement in 1666, having bought it of the Indians for the stereotyped collection of guns, blankets, knives, liquor, &c. Fifteen years afterward Newark had a population of 500 souls, and owned 10,000 acres of town lands and 40,000 acres of outlying plantations. In 1713 it was made a township by Queen Anne, but still its early growth was very slow and tedious, and in 1810 the population was less than 6,000. The *Sentinel of Freedom,* the oldest newspaper in the State of New-Jersey, its first number having been issued 5th October, 1796, gives the following census returns for 1810, in its number for 19th March, 1811:

Number of inhabitants in 1810 in the town plot of Newark, 4,388
Number of dwelling houses,   -   -   -   -   -   -   668
Number of stores, barns, stables, &c,   -   -   -   644

In those days the principal business of Newark and the other towns of Essex County was the manufacture of cloths, stuffs and general woolen goods, boots, shoes, and slippers, distilling and carriage-building. The value of the aggregate product of the country was only $1,210,471. To-day the manufacturing business of Newark alone is not less than $90,000,000 a year. The Board of Trade returns for 1871 give the number of manufacturing establishments at 1,015, the capital invested, $34,407,670; the number of hands employed, 29,147; the amount of wages paid, $14,767,257, and the value of the products $72,879,036.

*　　　*　　　*　　　*　　　*

With regard to the convenience of Newark as a place of residence for men doing business in New York, nice plots of land, 25 by 100, in desirable localities, for the erection of a house, can be bought for $2,000 to $2.500. Six to twelve-roomed houses, with every convenience and all the modern improvements, can be rented in the best parts of the city at from $500 to $800 a year.

*　　　*　　　*　　　*　　　*

The present area of the city of Newark is about 17½ square miles —11,200 acres, and the population is estimated at 125,000, of whom nearly 40,000, chiefly Germans and Irish, are foreigners. The valuation of real estate in the city, as assessed for 1871, is $62, 268,535, and of personal property, $21,717,806; together, $86, 986,341. The amount raised by taxation during the year was $1,396,620; and Newark can point with pride to the fact that this sum is only an increase of $3,966 over the taxation of 1870. Some of the local politicians must either be blind to opportunities, or else there can be no opportunities on which to seize. Here is a splendid opening for some coming Tweed.

Newark now boasts nine banks; though many of the business men here, having branch houses in New York, have also a banking account there. There are five savings banks, the oldest of which, the Newark Savings Institution, incorporated in 1847, has $12,022,844.56 deposits. The aggregate deposits of all the savings banks amount to $18,684,008.41. There are sixteen local life and fire insurance companies, with an aggregate capital of $3,723,817, and the Mutual Life Office of New York has a Newark branch.

*　　　*　　　*　　　*　　　*

As for the means of education the city seems comparatively rich. There are twenty-two public school houses, nine of which are each capable of accommodating from eight hundred to one thousand pupils, and have both primary and grammar departments : the other buildings are smaller and confined to one department. But, in addition, there are five evening schools, a Normal school, and a High school, under the charge of a principal and ten assistants, where the rising generation is prepared for commercial life or for college.

Foremost among the public institutions of interest in Newark is the New Jersey Historical Society. The settlement of New Jersey is coeval with the earliest history of this country, and it is therefore not surprising that the citizens of so conservative a State should have organized an institution the duty of whose officers it is "to discover, procure, and preserve, whatever relates to any department of the history of New Jersey, natural, civil, literary, or ecclesiastical, and generally of other portions of the United States." Besides being a depository for numerous curious and interesting relics of the past, many intimately connected with the romance of history, the Society's rooms contain the nucleus of a most valuable historical library. The collection already includes six thousand bound volumes, among which are twelve volumes of the minutes of the Long Parliament, and the *Sentinel of Freedom*, from its first issue, dated 5th October, 1796, down to the present day. The *Sentinel of Freedom* is the weekly edition of the Newark *Daily Advertiser*, which is by far the leading paper here, and which though forty years of age, appears to be in the heyday of its youth. The library also possesses ten thousand pamphlets, some of which are doubtless of little value, while others are equally valuable. There is too, a small collection of manuscripts, said to be of great value and rarity. This Historical Society, like those of New-York, Brooklyn. Boston, and other cities, is doing a work which men of cultured minds deeply regret was so neglected by their forefathers. They are collecting materials for some future Gibbon or Hallam, or even some brilliant, but untrustworthy, Macaulay, on which the coming History of the United States may be founded. And Newark boasts a Library Association, an incorporated stock institution, and therfore smelling of thirdrate works. But I am told that this is not so. Of course. I have had no time or opportunity to examine the contents of the shelves. But there is the best part of some eighteen or twenty thousand volumes; and, setting aside all assurances of their high character of literary works, there must be a goodly sprinkling of valuable literature somewhere on those shelves wherewith young Newark can enlighten and develop its budding mind. At all events, there are all the daily and weekly journals, the monthly magazines, and quarterly reviews; and there is "a little learning," if it be of the cramming order, to be gathered from them—at least the history of the day. And then if something austere is more congenial. there is the Young Men's Christian Association. with everything from prayer-meetings to lectures, and even entertainments in the Winter season. But if something more lively be desired, a distraction from the thoughts and cares of the daily life, something lighter than books, and yet not so frivolous as to be detrimental, there is the Newark Opera-House, which, thanks to the dramatic aspirations of Young America, and a constant influx of foreign mercenaries of the Thespian profession, is almost always tenanted by some star company of actors, or, if all other things fail, by a wandering troupe of minstrels. But there, again, the great railroad facilities of the city come in. If the *haut ecole* of young Newark think themselves above local performances. they can listen to Lucca's harmony in the New-York Academy of Music, cry over Miss Neilson's *Juliet*, or laugh themselves sore in the sides at Mr. Sothern's drollities, and yet catch the last train for home and sleep under the paternal roof. What would they have more?

APPENDIX B.

It was upon a cold, dark wintry night, near the close of the war, that a party of dauntless spirits, consisting of Capt. John Kidney, Capt. Henry Jaroleman, Jacob Garlaw, and Halmach Jaroleman, left their families and their firesides in search of adventure. A deep snow covered the Earth, and the howling wind gave admonition to all to remain within; but our party were bent on having prisoners that night. Having provided themselves with a pair of fleet horses, attached to a common wood sled, they left the neighborhood of the above village (Bloomfield) and laid their course toward the heights of Bergen. They soon arrived in the vicinity of the garrison, and leaving their horses tied to the fence they went on to reconnoitre. They returned shortly after, having ascertained that a school-house, some distance from the posts, was filled with officers and soldiers, rioting and dancing. Their plan of taking prisoners being matured, the company started with Kidney at their head. Coming upon the house, Kidney commenced giving his orders to his different divisions to surround the house, while he immediately forcing himself in at the door, took good care that his guard should show themselves and their bayonets at the threshold. Those within were struck with astonishment. "Every one of you are my prisoners," cried Kidney, "surrender, or you die." Having ordered them into line, he selected first a British officer, then a refugee, passed them along to the door, where they were muffled and hurried away to the sled; Kidney taking care to warn them that "the first one who attempted to escape, was a dead man." When they reached the meadows they heard the alarm gun fire, but they were too far for pursuit. The prisoners were secured in the Morristown jail, and our heroes returned well pleased with the night's adventure, leaving their prisoners much chagrined at the way they were taken.—*Barbour's Hist. Coll. N. Y.*

The Sales of Last Year!

NEW TRIUMPHS!

The Statistics from sworn returns of the Sales of Sewing Machines in 1872 (reported in 1873), show that the Singer Manufacturing Company sold, last year, over FORTY-FIVE THOUSAND more machines than ANY other Company, and over one quarter of all machines sold during that year.   Nine out of ten of said Singer Machines were for FAMILY use—proving the great popularity of the Singer in the household.   Annexed are the Sales of the different makers :

The Singer Manufacturing Company sold 219,758 Machines.

Wheeler & Wilson Manufacturing Company	174,088	"
Howe Machine Company (estimated)	145,000	"
Grover & Baker Sewing Machine Company	52,010	"
Domestic Sewing Machine Company	49,554	"
Weed Sewing Machine Company	42,444	"
Wilcox & Gibbs Sewing Machine Company	33,639	"
Wilson Sewing Machine Company	22,666	"
Amer. B. H. O. & Sewing Machine Company	18,930	"
Gold Medal Sewing Machine Company	18,897	"
Florence Sewing Machine Company	15,783	"
B. P. Howe Sewing Machine Company	14,907	"
Victor Sewing Machine Company	11,901	"
Davis Sewing Machine Company	11,376	"
Blees Sewing Machine Company	6,053	"
Remington Empire Sewing Machine Company	4,982	"
J. E. Braunsdorff & Co.	4,262	"
Keystone Sewing Machine Company	2,665	"
Bartlett Reversible Sewing Machine Company	1,000	"
Bartram & Fanton Manufacturing Company	1,000	"
Secor Sewing Machine Company	311	"

Orange Sporting Powder.

FOR SALE BY ALL PROMINENT DEALERS.

Orange Lightning Powder.

The best Powder made. Sizes, Nos. 1 to 7. Packed *only* in sealed one pound canisters.

☞ Care must be taken to use no finer size than No. 5 in metal shells or fine breech-loading guns, as it is too quick for the strength of either.

Orange Ducking Powder.

Expressly prepared for shooting water-fowl. Very strong and clean. Sizes, Nos. 1 to 5. Packed in metal ("gold band") kegs of $6\frac{1}{4}$ lbs., and canisters of 5 lbs. and 1 lb.

Audubon Powder.

Very quick, for woodcock and other shooting from muzzle-loading guns. Sizes, Nos. 1 to 4. Packed in metal kegs of $12\frac{1}{2}$ and $6\frac{1}{4}$ lbs., and canisters of 1 lb.

Orange Rifle Powder.

The best for *rifles*, and good for all ordinary purposes. Sizes, FG, FFG, and FFFG. Packed in wood and metal kegs of 25, $12\frac{1}{2}$, and $6\frac{1}{4}$ lbs., and canisters of 1 lb. and $\frac{1}{2}$ lb.

The above are the principal brands only, and will be found to give high velocity with less residuum than other Powders.

LAFLIN & RAND POWDER CO.

21 PARK ROW, NEW YORK.

Mining and Blasting Powders of all kinds. Dualin. Safety Fuse. Electric Blasting Apparatus. Steam Rock Drills, &c.